100 AMAZING FACTS ON THE AFRICAN PRESENCE IN THE BIBLE

List of Contributors

Graphic Artist:	Ben Kai Ben Israel
Copy Editors:	Zvenah Baht Yehuda
	Zehorah Baht Gavriel
Writers:	Eliyahu Ben Shaleak
	Raviyah Ben Israel
	Elyakeem Ben Shaleak
Researchers:	Aviahv Ben Boaz
	Elieet Baht Yessaschar
	Yafah Baht Israel
	Aturah Baht Israel
Computer Operations:	Courtesy of: Infinity Publishers
	Ahmahlyah Baht Rockameem
	Ahliel Ben Ahkeazer
	Moshay Ben Avidan
Project Coordinator:	Elyahshuv Ben Yehuda
Special Acknowledgment:	Dr. S.B. Yehuda, Hermeneutic Scholar and Dean, *The Institute of the School of the Prophets*, Jerusalem.

100 AMAZING FACTS ON THE AFRICAN PRESENCE *IN THE BIBLE*

"TO SOW THE FALLOW SOIL"

WINSTON-DEREK Publishers, Inc.

PENNYWELL DRIVE . P.O. BOX 90883 . NASHVILLE, TENNESSEE 37209

First printing 1992
Second printing 1993

The scriptural references used in this book are taken from the New Scofield Reference bible, 1967 ed.

OTHER REFERENCES:
The Black Biblical Heritage; 4000 years of African Biblical History, John L. Johnson, paperback, 310 pages, complete with illustrations and Bible references - $24.95

Bible Legacy of the Black Race: The Prophecy Fulfilled, Joyce Andrews, paperback, 225 pages with photographs and references - $11.95

PUBLISHED BY WINSTON-DEREK PUBLISHERS, INC.
Nashville, Tennessee 37205

Library of Congress Catalog Card No: 92-60787
ISBN: 1-55523-541-7

Printed in the United States of America

Dedication

These enlightening words are dedicated to the poor and the needy, the laymen of the earth, who are truly searching for another way.

> "Arise, shine; for thy light is come, and the
> glory of the Lord is risen upon thee.
>
> For, behold, the darkness shall cover the earth,
> and gross darkness the people; but the Lord
> shall arise upon thee, and his glory shall be
> seen upon thee."
>
> (Isaiah 60:1,2)

It is our fervent prayer that these words will be the light, within the gross darkness, that will guide your way unto the glory of the Lord.

Contents

INTRODUCTION

The tempestuous resentment about being denied as a people, a time, place and space in the historical drama of man, has been upgraded to a storm that cannot be held back. In this lifetime, we have witnessed the coming of a full circle: from the blatant racism that denied any African input into the creation of the world's greatest civilizations and man's finest achievements, to a recent flood of information revealing the common African ancestry of all people.

Recent newspaper and magazine articles have had no choice but to deal with man's true origins. This return to the truth has been dubbed as "Afrocentrism." Whole histories are being rewritten, major myths are being debunked and primary sources of thought are being reanalyzed in the wake of this storm. No stone has been left unturned.

And now, we point the finger to one of the last bastions of recreated histories, lost and stolen legacies and uninterrupted mistranslations and falsifications —the Holy Bible. As the truth is being told, we cannot leave out the Word of God, which has, over the centuries, inspired more than just the creation of the physical plane, but shapes the very soul of man.

The Bible is the greatest historical, prophetic compilation of God-inspired literature written by any men. This major work has been interpreted, defined and revised by numerous religious bodies and individuals. The true Word of God has eluded generation after generation. Men in "high places" have cunningly used the Bible as an instrument of deception. It is recorded in the prophetic writings of DANIEL 12:4,

> "But thou, O Daniel, shut up the words,
> and seal the book, even to the time of
> the end; many shall run to and fro; and
> knowledge shall be increased."

Thus, the truth of the book (the Bible) had been sealed until the time of the end. And now, in these last days, the seal has been loosened (REVELATIONS 5:5-6). In this work, "100 Amazing Facts on the African Presence in the Bible," we want to reveal the truth about the people of the Bible—their origins, their lands, their languages and cultures.

We have approached this great endeavor with a higher understanding of the "universal family" of man. In our presentation of the truth we remove all references to "race" in this text. It is a well-known fact that western world societies have fostered a deep-rooted sense of racism throughout the world.

Witness: Slavery, Jim Crow and segregation in the United States; apartheid in South Africa; the caste system in India; European exploitation of Africa and other lands south of the equator.

We have chosen not to buy into this myth. Yet, the truth remains: the roots of all modern men stem from the same African (Black) genesis. Consult or ask Bernal, Felder, Snowden, Van Sertima, Diop, Leakey, Herodutus, Josephus, Davidson, Godbey, Nietzsch, Wolpoff, Gould and a whole list of others. And now, add us to the list, because we have substantiated the African presence in this African Biblical genesis.

The book you have in your hands has been written to bring order to the confusion, truth to the lie and light to the darkness about the verity of the Bible.

Our first task is to use Biblical evidence, supportive academic references, and common sense logic and reasoning to show that the ancestral home of man (Adam), humanity's common ancestor, was in Africa, the land called Eden in the Bible.

We use the names Eden and Africa interchangeably and/or concurrently in order to maintain the reader's awareness that the two are really synonymous. Remember, the name "Africa" is actually of Latin origin and was imposed on that great continent by European explorers.

There is presently much controversy, fear and anger arising from the recent storm of Afrocentric revelations that state that the origins of life were in Africa (Eden). This anger has been surpassed only by the logical reality that accompanies it; i.e., if the origins of life were in the place called Africa, then the original occupant of this original place would have to be African/Edenic.

Only those who seek to remain in darkness will reject these truths. While on the other side, those who embrace these truths have been guaranteed to be set free and given everlasting life/light.

We know this truth about the African presence in the Bible will help everyone. The truth about the African presence in the Bible will set the record straight and give the descendants of those who made Biblical history a new sense of self, thus putting them on the path toward a better future. At the same time, it will give those who have worked arduously over the centuries, hiding the truth and creating lies, a much-needed rest.

In this spirit, we present "100 Amazing Facts on the African Presence in the Bible." We invite all purveyors of the truth—teachers, preachers and students—to utilize this work. Without a doubt, these "facts" will revolutionize your concept of yourself and the world around you. Please enjoy!

The original man, Adam, was formed, in the beginning, "from the dust of the earth" of the land of Africa/Eden. Thus, Adam, the progenitor of all men, was created from and in Africa/Eden (Genesis 2:7-8).

BIBLICAL CUSTOMS OF AFRICA

The real name for Africa is Eden! God planted a garden eastward in Eden. If Eden had an eastward direction, then logically it must follow that it had westward, northward and southward directions. The Bible stated this garden was located between the Nile River (Gihon), situated in Cush (Ethiopia), and the Euphrates River. Africa, in fact is a more recent term coined from the Latin language (Genesis 2:10-14).

The descendants of Jacob migrated to all parts of the world. Such tribes as the Fanti, Yoruba, Ashanti, Sudanese and Bantu are the descendants of Jacob's twelve sons. The Ashanti and Yoruba tribes of West Africa are direct descendants of the African/Edenic Hebrews, sharing many of the same cultural values (Genesis 49:1-33).

The African/Edenic tribe of Judah, largest of all in the house of Israel, was the last to be dispersed from the Holy Land in 70 A.D. Judah wandered in Africa for over a thousand years before most settled on the west coast of Africa, the point from which the Great Slave Trade to the Americas began. The land of the Ashanti in West Africa is one of the most important ancestral homes of the majority of African Americans (Genesis 49:1-33).

The Ashanti tribe of West Africa, whose ancestors were from the ancient African Hebrew Israelites divided themselves into 12 clans, very similar to the ancient 12 tribes of Israel (Genesis 49:1-28).

The Feast of Tabernacles, a holy day of the African Hebrew Israelites parallels the Ashanti Afahye Festival (Leviticus 23:34).

The holy day of Memorial Passover that is traditionally celebrated by the African Hebrews is also practiced today by the Falashas of Ethiopia. The Ethiopians consider themselves Beta-Israel (House of Israel), direct descendants of King Solomon and the Queen of Sheba, (an ancient land in Ethiopia). Called the "freedom festival" by these African/Edenic people, Passover is the most meaningful of all festivals for the Falashas, who understand that they are slaves in Ethiopia, awaiting the divine intervention that will take them to the land of Israel[1](Leviticus 23:5).

The order of the priesthood of the ancient African/Edenic Hebrews has many parallels to the priesthood of West African societies. For example, the priesthood of the Osene of the Ashanti tribe wear a breastplate divided into 12 parts similar to the ancient Hebrew Israelite priests. Both priesthoods have many of the same duties and privileges (Exodus 28:15).

The sprinkling of blood upon altars and door posts, a custom of the Ashanti tribe of West Africa follows, almost exactly, the ancient Hebraic tradition (Exodus 12:7).

The custom of offering sacrifices of domestic animals to the Creator finds its roots among ancient African/Edenic people. We also find that African Hebrew tribes emulated this practice in order to seek redemption from God[2,3](Leviticus 1:3).

Circumcision is a tradition that has been practiced in Africa for many millenniums. It is an Hebraic custom that is practiced throughout Africa, most notably in West Africa among the Ashanti and Yoruba (Genesis 17:9-10).

Hebrew customs, such as being set aside from physical contact with one's husband during the time of one's menstrual flow, and after childbirth, are practiced by the Ashanti tribe (Genesis 49:1-33).

The Ashantis of the Gold Coast forbade fighting on Saturday, the Hebrew Sabbath (Genesis 49:1-33).

Many Ashanti and Yoruba words have a Hebrew origin; (e.g. The word "Ashanti" has Hebraic origins. The word "ashan" in Hebrew means "smoke", and is the name of a town in ancient Israel belonging to the tribe of Judah. The "ti" means "my or mine". The term in Ashanti for "divine creator" is "bore-bore" and is the same as the Hebrew word for "creator" (Genesis 49:1-33).

Embalming is a process that was developed in African/Edenic culture. This process originated in Egypt and was adopted by the African/Edenic Hebrews during their stay in Egypt (Genesis 50:1).

The similarities in the socio-cultural aspects of childbirth and the importance of midwifery is comparable in the ancient civilizations of the Hebrew Israelites, Egyptians, and Mesopotamians. These same customs are still evident today in many parts of Africa among the various tribes. The use of birthing stools has long been associated with the traditional midwifery instruments. In the Fertile Crescent, "women very often crouched down in childbirth upon a pair of bricks or stones"[4](Exodus 1:15-21).

The true worship of God encompasses one's daily works and deeds. This is an African/Edenic concept, contrary to the popular belief worship should occur just one day out of the week. "We may conclude that there is no limit as to where and when African peoples perform one or more acts of worship. God is omnipresent, and He is 'reachable' at any time and any place people worship Him where and whenever the need arises"[5](Joshua 1:4).

RULERS, KINGS

In ancient African/Edenic civilization, the leader, king or chief was always referred to as being God's messenger in the midst of the people (Genesis 10:6, 16; Joshua 1:14, 16-18).

Og, an Amorite king of Bashan of the giant people of Ephraim had a powerful kingdom of sixty cities "fenced with high walls, gates and bars." The Amorites were a great African/Edenic people from the line of Ham (burnt, black) (Joshua 9:10).

Queen Jezebel was a beautiful Black woman from the city of Tyre of the Zidonians (Phoenicians). The Zidonians descended from Canaan's first son Zidon (I Kings 16:30-33).

Herod the Great, ruler of Judea, author of the decree to kill the male children during the time of Jesus' birth, was an Edomite (an African/Edenic people from the line of Esau/Isaac) whose father had converted following his country's defeat by Judea[6] (Matthew 2:1-21).

Uzziah, son and successor of King Amaziah, was a fourth generation descendent of Queen Jezebel. He ascended the throne at sixteen and built a nation strong both militarily and economically. The prince was known abroad for his success and inventions. He built large towers in Jerusalem that were well fortified. He was also noted for his agricultural techniques and his designs of machines that could throw arrows and stones through space[7] (II Chronicles 26:1).

All the ancient Pharaohs of Egypt were great African/Edenic kings The word Pharaoh means "great house." The Pharaoh was consid ered to be a god among his people (Genesis 41:46).

Cyrus, Darius and Artaxerus, kings of Persia, were descendants of the ancient seed of Shem. All of the people of this region were of African/Edenic origin. "The parts of the earth inhabited by the children of Shem were: parts of the territory of Assyria and Elam (Persia) east of the Tigris River, the eastern part of Syria, and parts of the Arabian peninsula. All the children of Shem were black"[8] (Ezra 6:14).

The Queen of Sheba, known as the Queen of Ethiopia and the Queen of the South, was from the Sheba province located in modern Yemen at the southern tip of the Arabian peninsula, across from Ethiopia. She was from the family line of Shem and Ham, a descendant of Abraham and Keturah (I Kings 10:1-13).

The great African/Edenic man Melchizedek which means "king of righteousness" was the first high priest of the city of "Salem," which later became Jerusalem. Melchizedek was part of the Messianic line (Genesis 14:18).

The Hammurabi Code was written by the great Black African/Edenic king Hammurabi (1792-1750 B.C.) of ancient Babylon. This code of law was the basis for the multitude of the laws that governed many of the great ancient African/Edenic civilizations of northeast Africa. The main principle of this code was "the strong shall not injure the weak." Portions of the Mosaic legal code are similar to the Hammurabi Code[9] (Genesis 21:9-34).

Photographs of reliefs of the great Pharaoh Rameses II indicate similarities comparable to the physical features and hairstyle of a modern Watusi warrior[10] (Exodus 1:11).

Joseph, one of the sons of Jacob, kidnapped by his own brothers and sol
to the Midianites, went on to become governor of the land of Egypt
When Joseph was reunited with his brothers years later, he was not recog
nized by them, proving that the people of this particular region were all o
the same physical family (Genesis chapters 37-42).

Moses, the African Hebrew lawgiver, was a Black man, verified when his hand was turned "white as snow" during his first encounter with ıe Holy Presence on Mt. Sinai. If Moses had already been white, his and could not have been turned "white as snow!" (Exodus 4:6-7).

PEOPLE

Methuselah, the world's longest living man, was an African/Edenic man from the family line of Enoch (a Black man). Methuselah lived to be 969 years old (Genesis 5:21-32).

The African/Edenic woman, Eve, created from the rib of Adam is the mother of all nations[11] (Genesis 2:21-24).

Joshua, the African Hebraic general, prayed unto God and made the sun and the moon stand still (Joshua 10:12, 13).

Nimrod, the "master hunter" and the grandson of Ham, was one of the world's first and foremost architects. He was the builder of the Tower of Babel and the City of Ur (Genesis 10:8-10).

The Chaldeans who were master astrologers and magicians, were an African people of Hamitic descent (Daniel 2:2).

Lazarus, as well as his sisters Mary and Martha, were African/Edenic people whose home, Bethany, lies close to Jerusalem on the road to Jericho. Bethany is also where John baptized[12,13] (John 11; 12:1).

Paul was an African/Edenic Hebrew Israelite from the tribe of Benjamin (Romans 11:1).

Daniel the prophet was a vegetarian. He asked to be fed only vegetables (pulses) and water. He refused to eat the King Nebuchadnezzar's meat (diet) or drink his wine (Daniel 1:4-16).

Simon the Cyrene, who helped Jesus bear the cross, was an African/Edenite from the line of Ham (Luke 23:26).

Saul, whose name later became Paul, and Barnabas were ordained by two Africans named Lucius from Cyrene and Simeon the Niger. These "chosen men of God . . . were teachers and prophets of an Antioch church located in Syria, about three hundred miles north of Jerusalem. They suffered threats and persecution following the crucifixion of Jesus, but chose to sustain themselves through their preaching . . ."[14] (Acts 11:19-29).

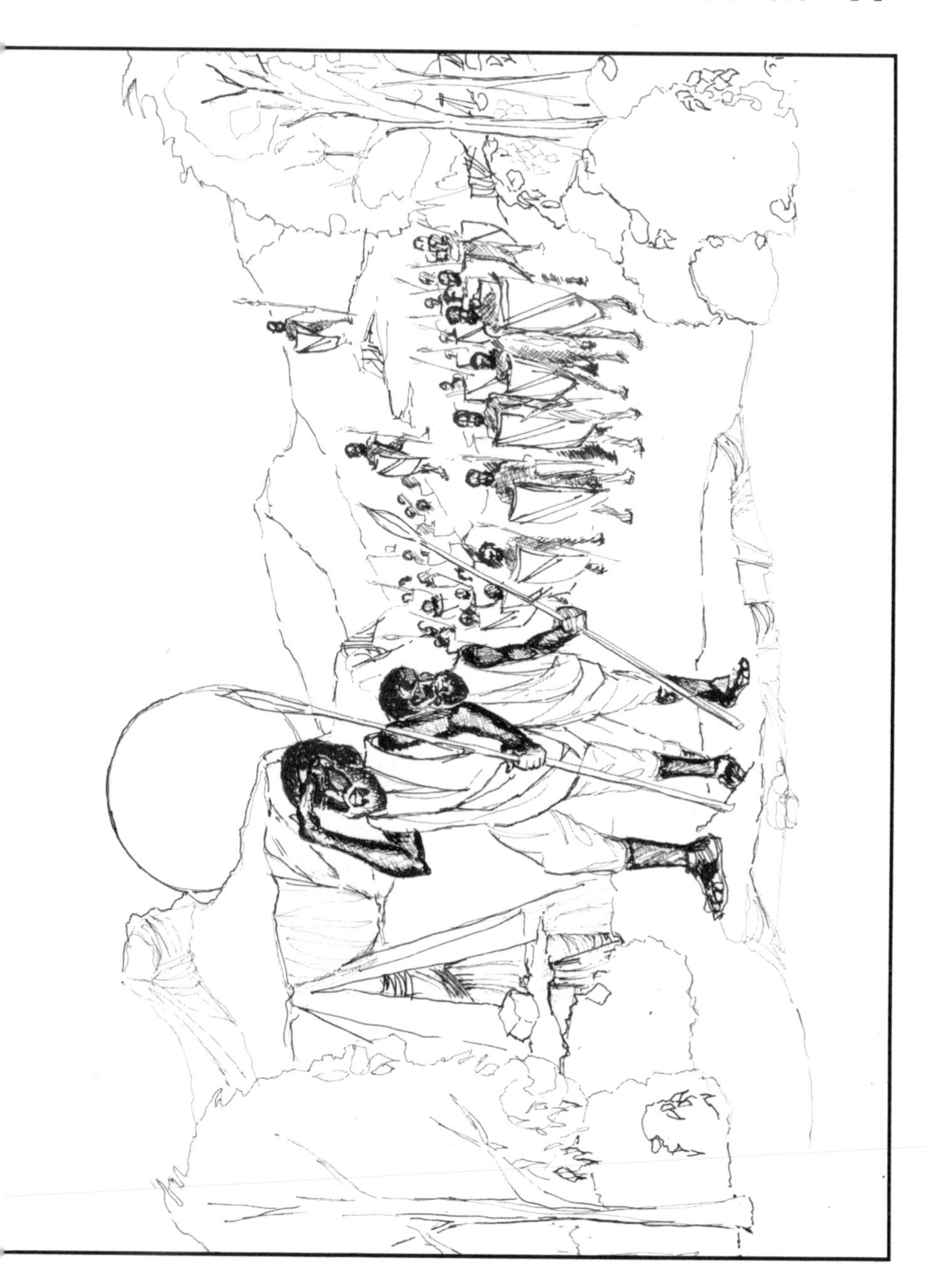

Only two African Hebrews, Joshua and Caleb, out of all of the adults from 20 years old and upward who left out of Egypt during the great Exodus, were allowed to enter into the Holy Land (Numbers 14:29-31).

The African/Edenic Hebrew, John the Baptist, was the cousin of Jesus (Matthew 1:18-25).

The Black Roman general, Titus, conquered and razed Jerusalem in 70 A.D. At that time the ruling African/Edenic Hebraic tribe, Judah, was exiled from the Holy Land, and did not return until 1969. (Destruction foretold: Luke 19:43, 21:20; Mark 13:2).

The names of the three Hebrew boys, Shadrach, Meshach and Abednego, were not their real names. These names were of the Chaldean tongue, given to them by their captors. Their Hebrew names were Azariah, Mishael and Hananiah. Similarly, African American slaves were given foreign names and a foreign language, to celebrate the civilization of Europe and denigrate Africa's former glory (Daniel 1:6).

The Midianites are considered to be one of the original Arab tribes. Many of their customs are in practice today among the nomadic tribes found in the desert north of the peninsula of Arabia. They are the descendants of Abraham and Keturah (Genesis 25:2-4).

Genealogy

Most people believe and accept the myth that Ham, the son of Noah, was cursed. The Bible, however, states that the curse was placed upon Canaan, a son of Ham. Ham had other sons, Mizriam (Egypt), Phut (Libya), Cush (Ethiopia). All of them were progenitors of African/Edenic people (Genesis 9:25-26; 10:6).

Abraham was an African Shemite. His name means "father of many nations." He is the progenitor of three important Black nations, the Israelites, Ishmaelites and Midianites (Genesis 17:20, 21; 25:2-4).

The original Arabs were Black! They were people of African/Edenic roots, who descended from the family line of Abraham (who was hemitic) and Hagar (who was Egyptian). Another line of Arabs escended from the union of Abraham and Keturah (who was Hamitic). his union took place when Abraham married Keturah, after the death of arah (Genesis 16:10-15; 25:1-2).

Contrary to popular myth, Shem, Ham, and Japheth (the three sons Noah) were all Black. Ham means hot, sunburnt. If one son w Black, all the sons were Black. One son could not be Black, the oth white and the third yellow, as prevalent arguments would have yc believe. Noah begat three sons from his "one wife", also Black. All Noah's sons had the same physical make-up, color and genealogical roo as their father and mother (Genesis 6:9-10).

Only eight African/Edenic people boarded the Ark that Noah built before The Flood. It was by them that the entire earth was replenished after The Flood. All of them were related either by blood or by marriage to Noah, an African/Edenic man. (Genesis 7:1-3; 8:15-17).

King Solomon, one of the great African/Edenic Hebrew kings, was from the family line of Shem and Ham. "Solomon, the king of Israel throughout Israel's finest years of prosperity, was a son and a successor to King David." His lineage can be scripturally traced as far back as Rehab, the Black Canaanite harlot, who was a descendant of Ham's fourth-born son, Canaan. Once again, we note: originally all Hamites and Shemites (or Semites) were Black[15] (Proverbs 1:1)

The Philistines were also a African/Edenic people from the family line of Ham (burnt, Black). Over the long years of conflict that the African Hebrews had with the Philistines the Hebrews were never able to totally subdue them[16] (Joshua 13:2).

The Amalekites were descendants of Amalek. His grandfather, Esau, was the brother of Jacob. They were the sons of Isaac, the son of Abraham, the African/Edenic patriarch. The Amalekites were an African/Edenic people from the line of Shem. They were great sailors, navigators and traders. They were among the first to send out explorers and set up colonies throughout the Mediterranean Sea area, even beyond the Straits of Gibraltar. They also left the legacy of their alphabetical system to the western world (II Samuel 1:8).

The Moabites were a Black people from the family line of Lot, the nephew of Abraham (a Black Shemite and descendant of Shem) (II Samuel 8:2).

Jesus descended from a Hamitic-Shemitic lineage extending back to the patriarch Abraham, spanning a total of 28 generations. The ironic reality in the Messiah's lineage, was that one of his ancestors, Rehab the Hamite, was an harlot! (Matthew 1:1-17).

GEOGRAPHY

The Nile, (known as the Gihon river in the Bible) passes through Uganda, the Sudan, and Egypt, extends from Lake Victoria (northern Kenya), all the way up to the Mediterranean Sea for a total of 3,485 miles. It is the longest river not only in Africa/Eden but in the world (Genesis 2:8-14)

The so-called "Middle East," or Asia Minor, is really northeast Africa. The Middle East and Africa were one land mass before being disconnected by the digging of the Suez Canal in 1869. The people of this region were all African/Edenic. They traveled, by land, between west and north Africa, northeast Africa, Asia and Europe (Genesis 42:1-3).

A natural cataclysmic upheaval began the severing of northeast Africa many eons ago when a massive earthquake created the Great Rift Valley, stretching from the Jordan Valley in the north to Mozambique in the south. The Red Sea is a major component of this great depression in the earth's structure. The region remains prone to earthquake activity (Zechariah 14:4-10).

The modern country of Iraq was originally a land of African/Edenic people. The region where Iraq is now located was originally called Babylonia. The great city of Babylon was established by Nimrod who descended from the family line of Ham (sunburnt, hot or black) (Genesis 10:6-9).

The city of Jerusalem, whose name translates into Hebrew to mean "inheritance of perfection" is one of the world's most famous cities. Located in northeast Africa, Jerusalem is the spiritual center for all the world's three major monotheistic religions, Christianity, Judaism and Islam (Joshua 15:7-8; 18:16).

The region of Mesopotamia, which included Assyria and Babylonia, was part of the location of the Garden of Eden. The people of this region were jet black Hamites and Shemites[17] (I Samuel 8:11).

Jesus lived in Africa/Eden, Israel, northeast Africa and Egypt, North Africa (Matthew 1:25; 2:13).

HEBRAIC TRANSLATIONS

In scripture where it is stated that the earth was "without form and void" it does not mean the world was empty. In Hebrew scripture instead of void the word "vohoo" (בֹּהוּ) is used which means chaos, confusion (Genesis 1:2; Jeremiah 4:23).

An angel is not a person that has wings and wears negligees. According to the African Hebraic word "mal-ahk" (מלאך),an angel is a messenger of God. That's why in Hebrews 13:1-2 we are told "Be not forgetful to entertain strangers: for thereby some have entertained angels unawares."

The name of Jesus in Hebrew is Ye-shu-ah, which means "one who shall save by righteous teachings and example" (Matthew 3:15).

The name John in Hebrew is Yo-ka-non which means "God bestows mercy" or "God is gracious and compassionate" (Matthew 3:1).

In the book of the Song of Solomon it is written that "Solomon was white and ruddy." The most accurate Hebraic rendering is that Solomon was "vibrant and manly" (a vibrant personality). Thus we find a description of his loveable character, not his skin color as insinuated. The English word "ruddy" was translated from the Hebrew word "adom" (אדום) whose root is "ah-dahm"(אדם)meaning man (Song of Solomon 5:10).

PHILOSOPHY

The proverbs of the Bible are a form of African/Edenic philosophy, wise sayings that speak to the relationship between life's daily events and God. The famous Aesop's (or Aethiop's) tales and parables are similar. The use of "proverbs" are a part of an African oral tradition that has been used for countless ages (Proverbs).

The scripture mentioning King Solomon's Shulamite bride is one of the few places in the Bible where color was an issue instead of cultural status. The scripture states, "I am Black, but comely." It is a pro-active response based on standards reflecting noble human and personhood values. This could be called the Biblical "I'm Black and I'm beautiful" statement[18] (Song of Solomon 1:5-6).

Christianity was spread throughout idolatrous Europe by African/Edenic people. The Cyrenians and Ethiopians, both African/Edenic peoples, were among the first to spread Christianity. (Acts 8:27, 37; I Chronicles 12:2; Acts 11:20).

The lamentations of Jeremiah parallel the African American "Blues". They were properly called "The Lamentations" because they spoke of the long, hard days in the field, the pain and the suffering. They were unique in that, to sing the "Blues," one did not need to have an outstanding voice. The songs and their manner of deliverance were truly a lament[19] (Lamentations).

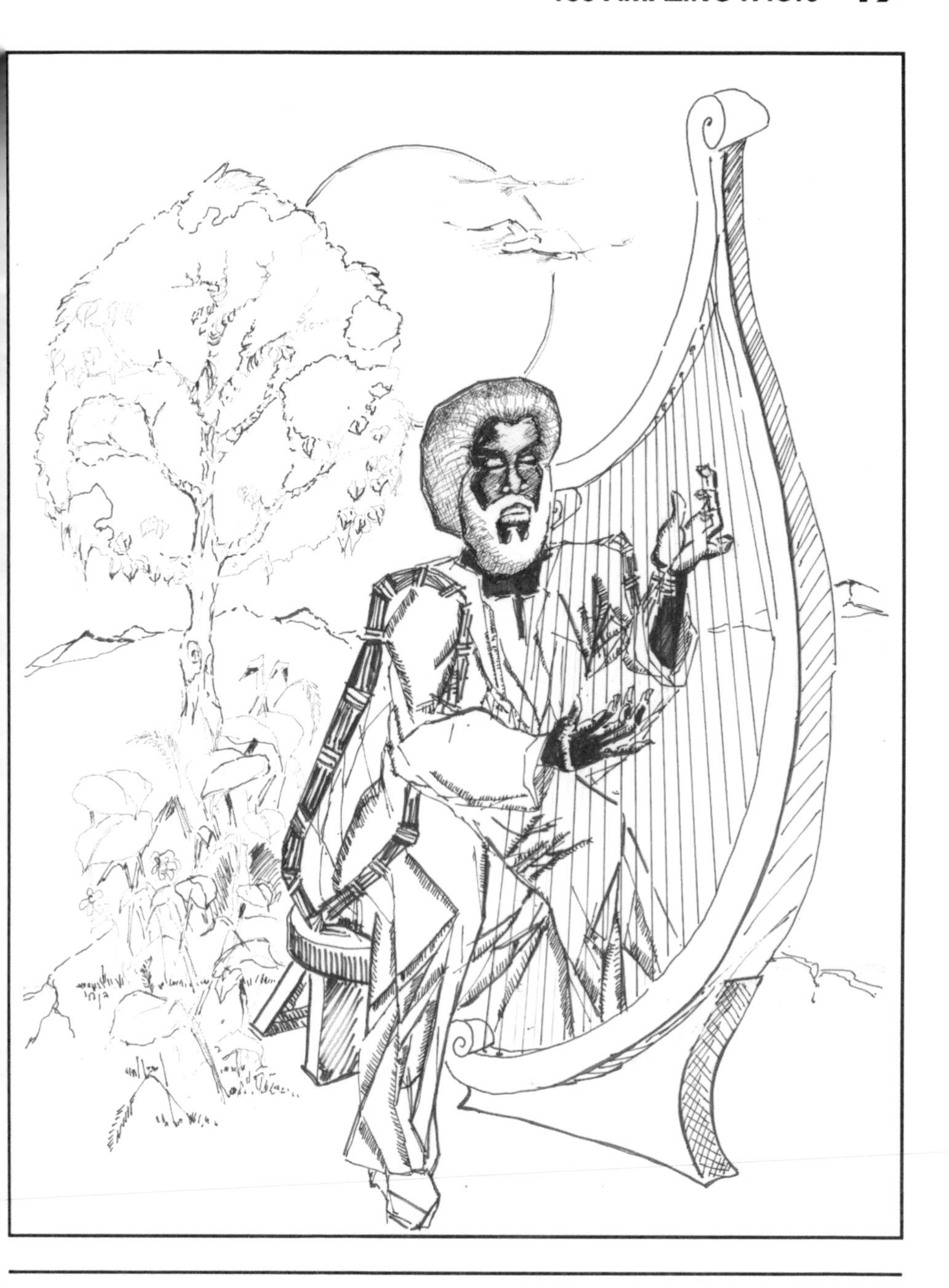

Jubal, an African/Edenic man who was the son of Lamech, the descendent of Cain, was the inventor of the harp and mouth organ. This invention allowed for the development of the principle of musical harmony. The harp became the national instrument of the Hebrews. It is still used widely throughout Africa in such tribes as the Malinke of Guinea and the Mbaka of Gabon. Music is important because it is much more than a form of entertainment. It identifies cultures, nationalities and communities. God is often worshiped through song in African/Edenic societies[20] (Genesis 4:21).

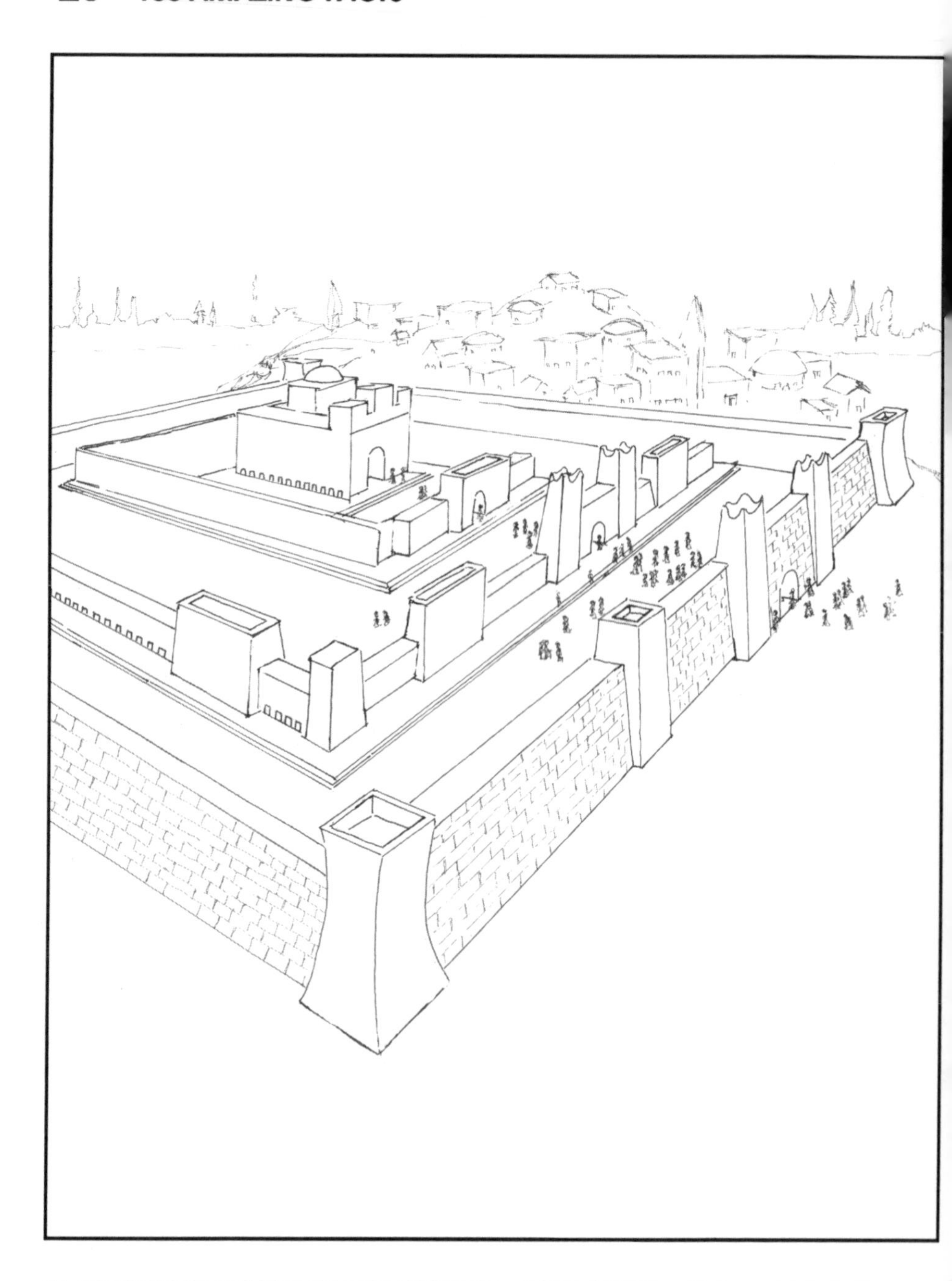

Solomon, the great African/Edenic King of Israel, designed one of the great architectural monuments the world has known. King Solomon built the Tem of God in Jerusalem without the sound of a hammer, axe, or any tool of iron dur the construction (I Kings 6:7).

INVENTIONS

The origin of the usage of trumpets by the U.S. Calvary and the U.S. Armed Forces can be traced to African/Edenic Hebrew tradition. An excellent example of the usage of trumpets was during the victory of the African/Edenic Israelites over Jericho (Joshua 6:4, 9, 16).

Chariots were an African/Edenic invention utilized prominently by Egyptians, Hebrews and other African nations of antiquity. Chariots contributed to the military power of a nation, evidence of which is found in early Biblical accounts of combat. Joseph, as a mark of distinction, was placed in the Egyptian Pharaoh's second chariot (Genesis 41:43).

The first masters of metallurgy were found in Africa as long as 4,000 years ago. The ancient African/Edenic Assyrians, Nubians and Egyptians even knew how to change iron into steel (I Samuel 13:19).

Solomon, the great African/Edenic King of Israel, designed one of the greatest architectural monuments the world has known. King Solomon built the Temple of God in Jerusalem without the sound of a hammer, axe, or any tool of iron during the construction (I Kings 6:7).

The architectural concept and design of pillars is an African/Edenic development, incorrectly identified as originating in Greece and Rome. The peoples of Africa/Eden had mastered many architectural feats centuries before Greece or Rome reached a technological peak in the development of their civilizations[21] (Judges 16:24).

AFRICAN AMERICAN ROOTS

Biblically, it was prophesied that the African/Edenic man would be brought to America in ships and sold as bondmen and bondwomen (Deuteronomy 28:68).

The African American concept of "soul brother" originated with King David and Jonathan because of the great, soulful love that they held for each other. Jonathan loved David as he loved his own soul (I Samuel 20:17).

The 430-year captivity of Israel, in ancient Egypt, almost exactly parallels the past physical and present spiritual captivity of the African American in the United States (Genesis 15:13).

The 430-year captivity of Israel in ancient Egypt almost exactly parall the past physical and continuing spiritual captivity of the Afric American in the United States (Genesis 15:13; Acts 7:6).

THINGS

Gopher wood, commonly used in shipbuilding and mentioned prominently in the Bible, is found in plentiful supply throughout the Fertile Crescent, in northeast Africa (Genesis 6:14-15).

Myrrh, the aromatic ingredient used in the holy anointing oil in Biblical times and burned as a popular incense today, is an indigenous African herb. It originated in Sheba, which is modern Yemen (Proverbs 7:17).

Frankincense furnished much wealth to the traders who traversed the spice routes from South Arabia to Gaza and Damascus. It was one of the ingredients of the holy anointing oil used by the Hebrew priest[22,23] (Exodus 30:34).

GENERAL INFORMATION

The predominant and characteristic form of leprosy in the Old Testament is a *white* variety covering the entire body or a large tract of its surface. Such were the cases of Moses, Miriam, Naaman and Gehazi."[24] (Exodus 4:6; Numbers 12:10; II Kings 5:1, 27).

The word "Bible" is derived from "biblicus/biblia" which is a Greek word from the name of the African papyrus plant which grew along the Nile during Biblical times. Papyrus, an aquatic plant growing in the Egyptian delta, was pressed into sheets of paper-like writing material and joined together to form a scroll. The oldest Biblical payprus fragments were found in 1947 among the Dead Sea Scrolls (dating from 250 B.C.E. to 50 C.E.)[25,26] (II John 12).

The world continues to marvel at the ancient intellect, wisdom, skill and wealth of the African/Edenic Hebrew King Solomon. King Solomon gave 200,000 bushels of wheat for food and over 170 gallons of pure oil annually to the household of King Hiram of Tyre in exchange for literally whole forests of cedar and fir trees, which he had skillfully navigated (by floating them) from Lebanon to Israel (I Kings 5:11).

The original governmental systems of African/Edenic people were without kings, chiefs, police forces and really without officials of any kind. Yet, they lived perfectly well with one another as long as foreigners did not interfere with them (Judges 18:1).

The Great Salt Sea is located in southern Israel, northeast Africa. It is the lowest point on earth. The Great Salt Sea is also known as the Dead Sea because no living organisms exist therein. As the lowest point on earth, it has a high concentration of salts and minerals as a result of the water run-off from the area's points above sea level. However, this sea is not without life because yearly thousands of tourists pay pilgrimage to the shores of the Great Salt Sea to take advantage of the beneficial and healing properties of its salt and mineral-laden waters for their skin (Jeremiah 17: 12-14).

One of the oldest civilizations in ancient times, of high order, was Sumer. The Biblical name for Sumer was Shinar. Nimrod, son of Cush (Ethiopia), was a mighty Ethiopian conqueror and builder in the land of Shinar. Sumer is the southern division of ancient Babylon. The Sumerians were ' the pre-Semetic population of the lower Euphrates Valley.' The 'pre-Semetic' means that the Black Sumerians were there first. These Sumerians or Ethiopians and their kindred appear to have settled along tracts from Mesopotamia to India.[27] (I Samuel 10:12).

The ancient city of Shechem was named after the son of Hamos, the Hivite, a descendent of Canaan, son of Ham. Today Shechem is known as Nablus (Genesis 34:2).

Before the rise of the Euro-gentile and the complete falling away from the laws and statutes of God, the African/Edenic mind knew no limits in its pursuits to develop and build. Nebuchadnezzar, an African/Edenic Hamite and King of Babylon, had built an image of solid gold that, equated to contemporary measurements, would have stood over ten stories high. This great golden image sparkled in the sun and could be seen from several kilometers away (Daniel 3:1).

The three wise men were African/Edenic kings. One, whose name was Gaspar, was king of African/Edenic India; Balthazar was king of Sheba (located south of Arabia); and the third Melchoir, (Melkon) was king of Persia[28-31] (Matthew 2:1).

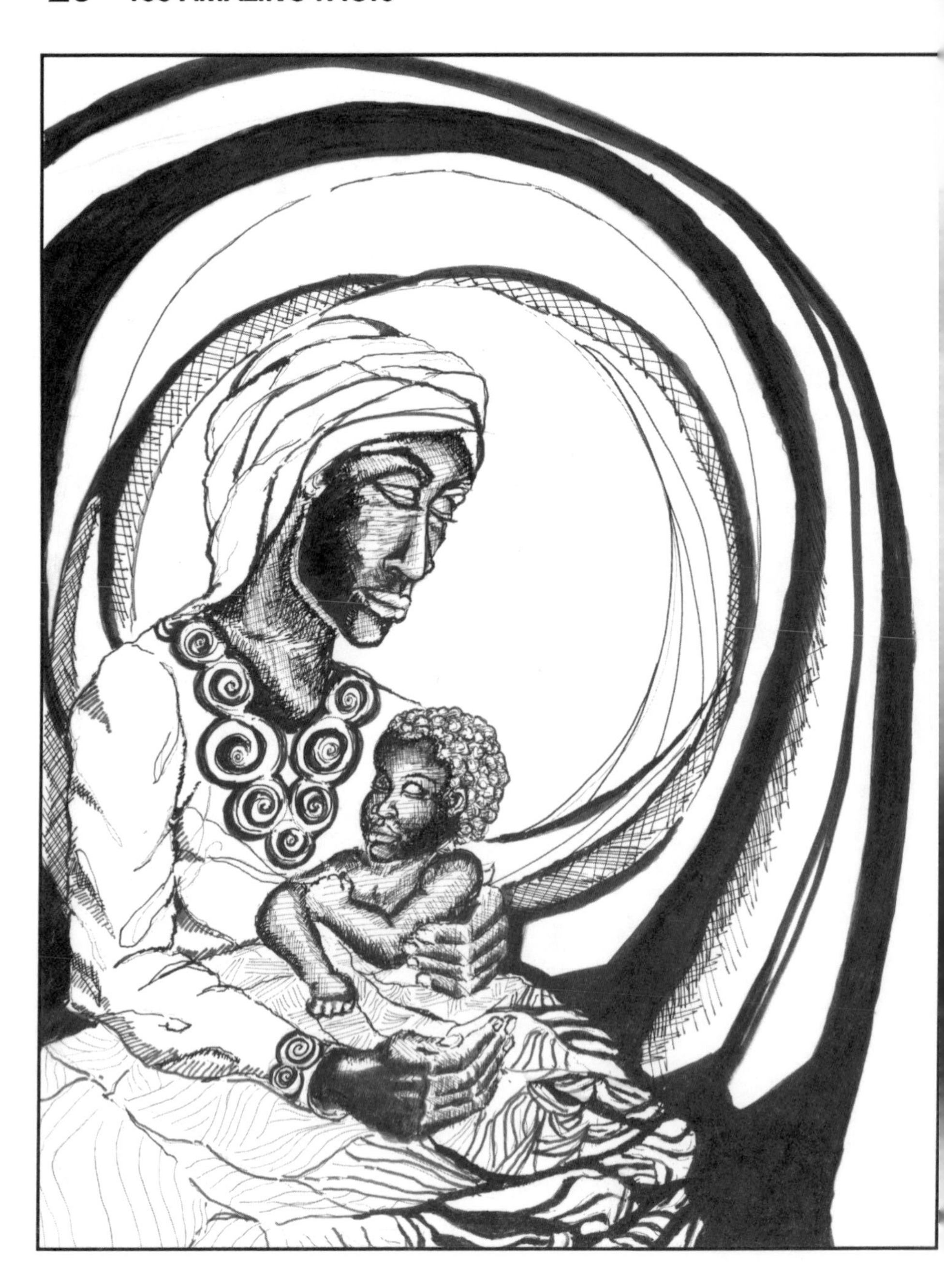

The image of the Virgin Mary and the baby Jesus, depicted as Black (African/Edenic), is held as sacred and is worshiped by the faithful throughout Europe. These images (paintings, sculptures, reliefs, etc.) can be found in Poland, Russia, Spain, Belgium, Switzerland and Czechoslovakia (Matthew 1:18-25).

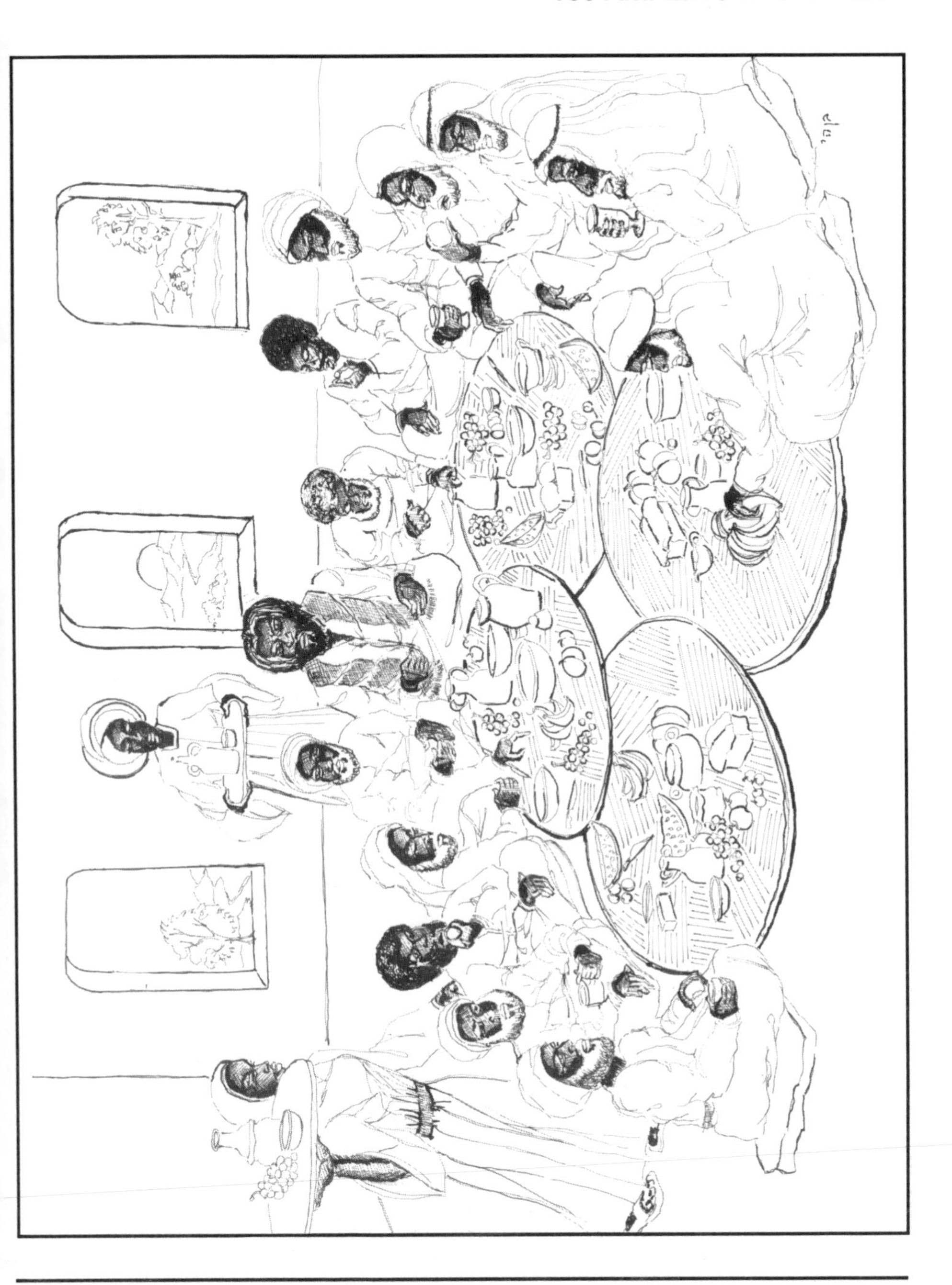

The Last Supper was a celebration of Passover, the Feast of Unleavened Bread. All of the disciples there were of African/Edenic descendancy (John 13:1).

Crucifixion is an ancient form of capital punishment that has its origin with the ancient people of Phoenicia and Persia, later adopted by the Romans. Jesus' enemies conspired to silence his message, handing down the sentence in order to publicly rebuke, humiliate and assassinate the Word of God. It placed him under an ancient curse, because it is written "cursed be anyone that be found hanged on a tree." This parallels what has taken place with leaders throughout the ages who have sought to truthfully stand on behalf of the people. The physical assassination of Mahatma Ghandi of India and Martin Luther King, Jr. of the United States and the character assassination of Nelson Mandela of South Africa are examples of modern physical and spiritual crucifixion (Matthew 27:33-50).

It was an African Hebraic custom of the ancient Nazarites, men consecrated unto God, not to cut their hair or shape their natural hair line. Samson's obedience to this custom was one of the sources of his strength. His disobedience led to his downfall at the hands of Delilah (Judges 13:5).

Lions, now found only in Africa below the Sahara, at one time were numerous in northeast Africa (Israel, Palestine) and are mentioned many times throughout the Bible. Israel's fauna is varied. "The leopard, hyena, polecat, wolf, jackal, coney, porcupine, antelope, ostrich, wild boar . . . many reptiles . . . the ibex . . . the hyrax are just a few of the many varieties of animal life, including 70 mammal, 80 reptile and eight amphibia species found here." This wealth of animal life is "due to its position at the junction of three natural zones"[32,33] (Jeremiah 49:19; Isaiah 5:39; I Samuel 17:34-35; Daniel 6:16-23).

There are many plants and spices used today that have their origins in the Bible lands and that were used during Biblical times. For example, the coriander plant grows wild in Palestine (Israel) and Egypt. It is a spicy grey and white seed used during the time of Moses. The flax seed was cultivated by African Egyptians before the Exodus and before the conquest by the Canaanites. Flax is one of the world's oldest textile fibers, used in the making of varying textures of linen. The plant grows to a height of three feet and produces beautiful blue flowers. Linseed oil, used as a wood preserver, comes from the pod of the flax plant. The wise African/Edenic King Solomon was also a learned botanist who collected plants from all over the world and brought them to Israel to study and grow. In Israel, northeast Africa, 2,500 plant types can be found, including 150 indigenous species.[34] (Exodus 16:31; Hosea 2:5, 9; Joshua 2:6; Isaiah 19:9).

Some African Hebraic Translations of the Books of the Bible:

EXODUS (SHMOTE): שׁמוֹת
"Names"—attributes that characterize the existence of God.

NUMBERS (BAH MEEDBAR): במדבר
"In the wilderness."

JOSHUA (YIHOSHAWAH): יהוֹשׁע
"And He shall save"—relating to God saving the children of Israel as they entered into the Promised Land at the crossing of the Jordan River at Jericho.

JUDGES (SHOF-TEEM): שׁוֹפטים
"Judges"—Deliverers who had to exercise the Judgment of God (intelligence of God) in their rule of the children of Israel and to ensure the defeat of their enemies.

SAMUEL (SHMOOEL): שׁמוּאל
"His name is of God" or "one who possesses the attributes or characteristics of God."

ISAIAH (YISHIYAH): ישׁעיה
"And He shall save" or "God shall deliver from condemnation; the salvation or redemption of God (Righteousness)."

MATTHEW (MAHTEE): מתי
"Gift of God."

NOTES

1. Louis Rapaport, *The Lost Jews* (New York: Stein and Day, 1983), 16.
2. Joseph J. Williams, *Hebrewisms of West Africa* (New York: Biblo and Tannen, 1967), 89.
3. John S. Mbiti, *African Religions and Philosophy* (Nairobi: Heineman International, 1990), 58, 821.
4. J. D. Douglas, ed., *The New Bible Dictionary* (Grand Rapids, Michigan: Wm. B. Eerdmans), s.v. "midwife."
5. Mbiti, *African Religions and Philosophy*, 73.
6. Madeline S. Miller and J. Lane Miller, eds., *Harper's Encyclopedia of Bible Life* (London: Harper and Row, 1978), s.v. "Herod the Great."
7. John L. Johnson, *The Black Biblical Heritage* (Nashville: Winston-Derek, 1988), 163.
8. Rudolph A. Windsor, *From Babylon to Timbuktu* (Philadelphia: Windsor's Golden Series Publications, 1988), 19.
9. *The Interpreter's Dictionary of the Bible*, vol. 2, s.v. "Hammurabi."
10. Cheikh Anta Diop, *The African Origin of Civilization*, ed. and trans. Mercer Cook (Chicago: Lawrence Hill, 1974), 19, 43, 78.
11. John Tierney with Lynda Wright and Karen Springen, "The Search for Adam and Eve," *Newsweek*, 11 January 1988.
12. *Smith's Bible Dictionary*, revised edition, s.v. "Bethany."
13. Douglas, *The New Bible Dictionary*, s.v. "Bethany."
14. Johnson, *The Black Biblical Heritage*, 211.
15. Ibid., 123.
16. *Smith's Bible Dictionary*, s.v. "Philistines."
17. Windsor, *From Babylon to Timbuktu*, 13.
18. Rev. Walter A. McCray, *The Black Presence in the Bible*, vol. 1 (Chicago: Black Light Fellowship, 1990), 33.
19. Ben Ammi, *God, the Black Man and Truth* (Washington, D.C.: Communicators Press, 1990), 33.
20. J. H. Kivabena Nketia, *The Music of Africa* (London: W. W. Norton, 1974), 104.
21. Janet S. Garber, ed., *The Concise Encyclopedia of Ancient Civilizations* (London: Franklin Watts, 1978), 52.
22. Douglas, ed., *The New Bible Dictionary*, s.v. "Frankincense."
23. Williams, *Hebrewisms*, 175.

24. *Smith's Bible Dictionary*, s.v. "Leper, Leprosy."
25. Johnson, *The Black Biblical Heritage*, 237.
26. Watson E. Mills, gen. ed., *Mercer Dictionary of the Bible* (Macon, GA: Mercer Univ. Press, 1990), s.v. "Papyrus."
27. Windsor, *From Babylon to Timbuktu*, 15–17.
28. *The Interpreter's Dictionary of the Bible*, vol. 2, s.v. "Gaspar."
29. Ivan Van Sertima and Runoko Rashidi, *African Presence in Early Asia* (London: Transaction Publishers, 1988), 82–83, 236–237.
30. Johnson, *The Black Biblical Heritage*, 199.
31. Van Sertima and Rashidi, *African Presence in Early Asia*, 8, 55.
32. Neil Tilbury, *Israel: A Travel Survival Kit* (Victoria, Australia: Lonely Planet, 1989), 27–28.
33. Trent C. Butler, *Holman Bible Dictionary*, (Nashville: Holman Bible Publishers, 1991), 57.
34. Tilbury, *Israel, A Travel Survival Kit*, 28.

GOD, THE BLACK MAN AND TRUTH

BEN AMMI

$15.00 PB ISBN 0-9620463-1-0

In *God, the Black Man and Truth*, Ben Ammi gives light to the disheartening realization that we are a people buried in the muck and mire of complacency; a people imprisoned in poverty and ignorance and trapped in the web of religion. *God, the Black Man and Truth* underscores the need for our people to ignite the fires of discontent—this time with new fuel—for it is beyond the time for righteous men to sit idly as the wicked prevail, unmolested in their den of iniquity.

THE MESSIAH AND THE END OF THIS WORLD

BEN AMMI

$17.00 PB ISBN 0-9620463-3-7

Ben Ammi brings God down from the sky (the abstract) where the theological teachings of Europe have transplanted Him. In doing so, he causes us to see evermore clearly the "path" that leads to God and the proper way to develop a harmonious relationship with Him. He gives us the keys which will ultimately influence the realization of the absolute life, the life which only a minute few of the world's inhabitants, past and present, have ever experienced. They are the keys to the world to come . . . with the end of *this* world.